50 Queen Royal Recipes

By: Kelly Johnson

Table of Contents

- Queen's Coronation Chicken
- Royal Victoria Sponge Cake
- Duchess Lemon Drizzle Cake
- Buckingham Palace Scones
- Queen's Afternoon Tea Sandwiches
- Royal Roast Beef with Yorkshire Pudding
- Windsor Castle Trifle
- Crown Jewel Salmon en Croûte
- Queen's Favorite Chocolate Biscuit Cake
- Earl Grey Infused Shortbread
- Royal Garden Party Cucumber Sandwiches
- Balmoral Venison Stew
- Queen's Favorite Scrambled Eggs
- Coronation Prawn Cocktail
- Royal English Pea Soup
- Lavender Honey Glazed Roast Chicken
- The Queen Mother's Favorite Fish Pie
- St. James's Potted Shrimp
- Princess Grace's Champagne Jelly
- Clarence House Apple Crumble
- Royal Banoffee Pie
- Kensington Palace Lemon Posset
- Duke of Edinburgh's Grilled Lamb Chops
- Majestic Gooseberry Fool
- Queen's Favorite Dover Sole Meunière
- Prince of Wales Welsh Rarebit
- Queen's Signature Gin and Dubonnet
- Royal Family's Smoked Salmon Blinis
- Queen's Personal Tomato Salad
- Grand Royal Beef Wellington
- Princess Diana's Bread and Butter Pudding
- Regal Sticky Toffee Pudding
- The Crown's Mulled Wine
- Queen's Garden Mint Pea Risotto
- Buckingham Palace Fruitcake

- The Royal Eton Mess
- Princess Margaret's Crêpes Suzette
- Highgrove Estate Honey & Oat Bars
- Balmoral Castle Venison Wellington
- Queen's Champagne and Strawberry Sorbet
- King's Coronation Lamb Curry
- Queen's Royal Game Pie
- Crown Jewel Pavlova
- Princess Anne's Favorite Kedgeree
- Royal Cheese Soufflé
- Duchess of Cambridge's Pumpkin Soup
- Windsor Park Asparagus Tart
- The Royal Family's Christmas Pudding
- Monarch's Heritage Plum Cake
- Queen's Signature Afternoon Tea Blend

Classic Coronation Chicken

Ingredients

- 2 cooked chicken breasts, shredded or diced
- 2 tbsp mayonnaise
- 2 tbsp Greek yogurt (or crème fraîche)
- 1 tsp mild curry powder
- 1 tbsp mango chutney
- 1 tbsp sultanas (optional)
- 1 tbsp flaked almonds (optional)
- ½ tsp lemon juice
- Salt and pepper, to taste

Instructions

1. In a bowl, mix mayonnaise, Greek yogurt, curry powder, mango chutney, lemon juice, salt, and pepper until well combined.
2. Stir in the cooked chicken, ensuring it is evenly coated.
3. Add sultanas and flaked almonds, if using.
4. Serve chilled in sandwiches, on a jacket potato, or with a salad.

Royal Victoria Sponge Cake

Ingredients

- 200g unsalted butter, softened
- 200g caster sugar
- 4 large eggs
- 200g self-raising flour
- 1 tsp vanilla extract
- 2 tbsp milk
- 200g strawberry jam
- 200ml double cream, whipped
- Icing sugar, for dusting

Instructions

1. Preheat the oven to 180°C (350°F). Grease and line two 20cm cake tins.
2. Cream together butter and sugar until fluffy.
3. Beat in eggs one at a time, then fold in flour and vanilla extract. Add milk if needed.
4. Divide the batter evenly between the tins and bake for 20-25 minutes until golden.
5. Let cakes cool, then spread jam and whipped cream over one layer. Place the second sponge on top.
6. Dust with icing sugar before serving.

Duchess Lemon Drizzle Cake

Ingredients

- 225g unsalted butter, softened
- 225g caster sugar
- 4 large eggs
- 225g self-raising flour
- Zest of 2 lemons
- Juice of 1 lemon

For the drizzle:

- 100g granulated sugar
- Juice of 1 lemon

Instructions

1. Preheat oven to 180°C (350°F). Grease and line a loaf tin.
2. Beat butter and sugar together until light. Add eggs one at a time, then fold in flour and lemon zest.
3. Pour batter into the tin and bake for 40-45 minutes until golden.
4. Mix lemon juice and sugar for the drizzle. Poke holes in the warm cake and pour over the drizzle.
5. Let cool before serving.

Buckingham Palace Scones

Ingredients

- 350g self-raising flour
- 85g unsalted butter, cubed
- 3 tbsp caster sugar
- 175ml whole milk
- 1 tsp vanilla extract
- 1 beaten egg (for glazing)

Instructions

1. Preheat oven to 220°C (425°F). Line a baking tray.
2. Rub butter into flour until the mixture resembles breadcrumbs. Stir in sugar.
3. Warm milk slightly, add vanilla, then mix into the flour mixture to form a soft dough.
4. Roll out to 2cm thick, cut into rounds, and place on the tray. Brush with egg.
5. Bake for 12-15 minutes until golden.
6. Serve warm with clotted cream and jam.

Queen's Afternoon Tea Sandwiches

Cucumber & Cream Cheese Sandwiches

Ingredients

- Soft white bread, crusts removed
- Cream cheese
- Thinly sliced cucumber
- Salt and pepper

Instructions

1. Spread cream cheese on bread, layer cucumber slices, season lightly, and sandwich together.

Smoked Salmon & Dill Sandwiches

Ingredients

- Soft wholegrain bread
- Smoked salmon
- Cream cheese
- Fresh dill

Instructions

1. Spread cream cheese on bread, layer smoked salmon, sprinkle dill, and sandwich together.

Egg & Cress Sandwiches

Ingredients

- Soft white bread
- 2 boiled eggs, mashed
- 1 tbsp mayonnaise
- Fresh cress

Instructions

1. Mix eggs with mayonnaise, spread on bread, sprinkle cress, and sandwich together.

2. Cut all sandwiches into fingers or triangles before serving.

Royal Roast Beef with Yorkshire Pudding

Ingredients

For the Roast Beef:

- 1.5kg beef rib roast
- 2 tbsp olive oil
- 2 tsp salt
- 1 tsp black pepper
- 1 tsp English mustard
- 2 sprigs fresh rosemary

For the Yorkshire Pudding:

- 150g plain flour
- 3 eggs
- 200ml whole milk
- ½ tsp salt
- 2 tbsp beef dripping or vegetable oil

Instructions

1. Preheat oven to 220°C (425°F). Rub beef with oil, salt, pepper, and mustard. Place in a roasting tin with rosemary.
2. Roast for 20 minutes, then reduce temperature to 180°C (350°F) and cook for 50-60 minutes. Rest for 20 minutes before carving.
3. For Yorkshire pudding, whisk flour, eggs, milk, and salt until smooth. Let batter rest for 30 minutes.
4. Heat beef dripping in a muffin tin at 220°C (425°F) until smoking hot.
5. Pour batter into hot tins and bake for 20-25 minutes until golden and risen.

Windsor Castle Trifle

Ingredients

- 1 Madeira sponge cake, sliced
- 200ml sherry or fruit juice
- 250g mixed berries
- 500ml custard
- 300ml double cream, whipped
- 50g flaked almonds, toasted

Instructions

1. Layer sponge cake in a trifle dish and drizzle with sherry or juice.
2. Add a layer of mixed berries, followed by custard.
3. Top with whipped cream and sprinkle with almonds. Chill before serving.

Crown Jewel Salmon en Croûte

Ingredients

- 1 salmon fillet (500g)
- 1 sheet puff pastry
- 100g spinach, wilted
- 50g cream cheese
- 1 egg, beaten
- Salt and pepper

Instructions

1. Preheat oven to 200°C (400°F). Roll out puff pastry.
2. Mix spinach and cream cheese, season, and spread over salmon.
3. Wrap salmon in pastry, sealing edges. Brush with beaten egg.
4. Bake for 25-30 minutes until golden brown.

Queen's Favorite Chocolate Biscuit Cake

Ingredients

- 200g digestive biscuits, broken
- 100g butter, melted
- 200g dark chocolate
- 2 tbsp golden syrup
- 1 tbsp cocoa powder

Instructions

1. Melt butter, chocolate, and syrup together. Stir in cocoa.
2. Mix with biscuits and press into a lined tin.
3. Refrigerate for at least 2 hours before slicing.

Earl Grey Infused Shortbread

Ingredients

- 250g plain flour
- 100g caster sugar
- 200g butter, cold and cubed
- 2 Earl Grey tea bags, leaves only

Instructions

1. Preheat oven to 180°C (350°F).
2. Rub butter into flour and sugar, add tea leaves, and mix into a dough.
3. Roll out and cut into shapes.
4. Bake for 12-15 minutes until golden.

Royal Garden Party Cucumber Sandwiches

Ingredients

- Soft white bread, crusts removed
- Cream cheese
- Thinly sliced cucumber
- Salt and pepper

Instructions

1. Spread cream cheese on bread, layer cucumber slices, season lightly, and sandwich together.
2. Cut into fingers or triangles before serving.

Balmoral Venison Stew

Ingredients

- 500g venison, diced
- 1 onion, chopped
- 2 carrots, sliced
- 2 cloves garlic, minced
- 500ml beef stock
- 200ml red wine
- 1 sprig thyme
- 1 bay leaf

Instructions

1. Brown venison in a pot. Remove and set aside.
2. Sauté onion, carrots, and garlic until softened.
3. Return venison to the pot, add stock, wine, thyme, and bay leaf.
4. Simmer for 2 hours until tender.

Queen's Favorite Scrambled Eggs

Ingredients

- 4 eggs
- 2 tbsp butter
- 2 tbsp cream
- Salt and pepper

Instructions

1. Whisk eggs and cream together.
2. Melt butter in a pan over low heat.
3. Cook eggs slowly, stirring continuously until soft and creamy.

Coronation Prawn Cocktail

Ingredients

- 200g cooked prawns
- 2 tbsp mayonnaise
- 1 tbsp mango chutney
- 1 tsp mild curry powder
- ½ tsp lemon juice

Instructions

1. Mix mayonnaise, chutney, curry powder, and lemon juice.
2. Stir in prawns and serve in lettuce cups or with toast.

Royal English Pea Soup

Ingredients

- 500g fresh or frozen peas
- 1 onion, chopped
- 1 garlic clove, minced
- 500ml vegetable stock
- 100ml cream

Instructions

1. Sauté onion and garlic in a pan until soft.
2. Add peas and stock, simmer for 10 minutes.
3. Blend until smooth, stir in cream, and season to taste.

Lavender Honey Glazed Roast Chicken

Ingredients

- 1 whole chicken (1.5-2kg)
- 3 tbsp honey
- 1 tbsp dried lavender
- 2 tbsp olive oil
- 2 cloves garlic, minced
- 1 tsp salt
- ½ tsp black pepper
- 1 lemon, halved
- Fresh thyme sprigs

Instructions

1. Preheat oven to 190°C (375°F).
2. Mix honey, lavender, olive oil, garlic, salt, and pepper.
3. Place lemon halves and thyme inside the chicken.
4. Brush chicken with honey-lavender mixture.
5. Roast for 75-90 minutes, basting occasionally, until golden and cooked through.

The Queen Mother's Favorite Fish Pie

Ingredients

- 500g mixed white fish and smoked haddock
- 200g prawns
- 500ml milk
- 50g butter
- 50g flour
- 1 tsp mustard
- 100g cheddar, grated
- 4 potatoes, mashed
- Salt and pepper

Instructions

1. Preheat oven to 180°C (350°F).
2. Poach fish in milk, then flake into a baking dish.
3. Melt butter, stir in flour, then gradually add poaching milk to make a sauce.
4. Stir in mustard, cheese, and season. Pour over fish and top with mashed potatoes.
5. Bake for 30 minutes until golden.

St. James's Potted Shrimp

Ingredients

- 200g brown shrimp
- 100g butter
- ½ tsp mace
- ½ tsp cayenne pepper
- Salt and pepper

Instructions

1. Melt butter, stir in shrimp and spices, then season.
2. Spoon into ramekins and refrigerate until set.
3. Serve with warm toast.

Princess Grace's Champagne Jelly

Ingredients

- 250ml champagne
- 100ml white grape juice
- 50g sugar
- 3 gelatine leaves

Instructions

1. Soak gelatine in cold water until soft.
2. Heat grape juice and sugar, then dissolve gelatine in it.
3. Stir in champagne, pour into glasses, and chill until set.

Clarence House Apple Crumble

Ingredients

- 4 apples, peeled and sliced
- 50g sugar
- 100g flour
- 75g butter
- 50g brown sugar

Instructions

1. Preheat oven to 180°C (350°F).
2. Place apples in a baking dish and sprinkle with sugar.
3. Rub butter into flour and brown sugar until crumbly.
4. Scatter over apples and bake for 30 minutes.

Royal Banoffee Pie

Ingredients

- 1 digestive biscuit base
- 1 tin condensed milk (dulce de leche)
- 2 bananas, sliced
- 300ml whipped cream
- Chocolate shavings

Instructions

1. Spread dulce de leche over the biscuit base.
2. Layer banana slices and top with whipped cream.
3. Sprinkle with chocolate shavings.

Kensington Palace Lemon Posset

Ingredients

- 300ml double cream
- 75g sugar
- 1 lemon, juiced

Instructions

1. Heat cream and sugar until dissolved, then remove from heat.
2. Stir in lemon juice and pour into ramekins.
3. Chill for at least 3 hours before serving.

Duke of Edinburgh's Grilled Lamb Chops

Ingredients

- 4 lamb chops
- 2 tbsp olive oil
- 1 tbsp rosemary, chopped
- 2 cloves garlic, minced
- Salt and pepper

Instructions

1. Rub lamb chops with oil, rosemary, garlic, salt, and pepper.
2. Grill for 3-4 minutes per side until cooked to preference.

Majestic Gooseberry Fool

Ingredients

- 300g gooseberries
- 50g sugar
- 300ml whipped cream

Instructions

1. Cook gooseberries with sugar until soft, then cool.
2. Fold into whipped cream and serve chilled.

Queen's Favorite Dover Sole Meunière

Ingredients

- 2 Dover sole fillets
- 50g butter
- 1 lemon, juiced
- 2 tbsp flour
- Salt and pepper

Instructions

1. Dredge sole in flour, season, and fry in butter until golden.
2. Drizzle with lemon juice before serving.

Prince of Wales Welsh Rarebit

Ingredients

- 250g mature cheddar, grated
- 2 tbsp butter
- 2 tbsp flour
- 100ml beer (or milk)
- 1 tsp English mustard
- 1 tsp Worcestershire sauce
- 2 egg yolks
- 4 slices of toasted bread

Instructions

1. Melt butter in a pan, stir in flour, and cook for 1 minute.
2. Gradually add beer, whisking until smooth.
3. Add mustard, Worcestershire sauce, and cheese, stirring until melted.
4. Remove from heat, stir in egg yolks, and spread over toast.
5. Grill until bubbling and golden.

Queen's Signature Gin and Dubonnet

Ingredients

- 50ml Dubonnet
- 25ml gin
- Ice cubes
- Lemon slice

Instructions

1. Fill a glass with ice.
2. Pour in Dubonnet and gin.
3. Stir gently and garnish with a lemon slice.

Royal Family's Smoked Salmon Blinis

Ingredients

- 12 blinis
- 100g smoked salmon
- 100g crème fraîche
- 1 tsp lemon juice
- 1 tsp horseradish
- Fresh dill

Instructions

1. Mix crème fraîche, lemon juice, and horseradish.
2. Top each blini with a dollop of the mixture and a piece of smoked salmon.
3. Garnish with fresh dill.

Queen's Personal Tomato Salad

Ingredients

- 4 heirloom tomatoes, sliced
- 1 small red onion, thinly sliced
- 2 tbsp olive oil
- 1 tbsp balsamic vinegar
- Salt and pepper
- Fresh basil

Instructions

1. Arrange tomatoes and onions on a plate.
2. Drizzle with olive oil and balsamic vinegar.
3. Season with salt and pepper, then garnish with basil.

Grand Royal Beef Wellington

Ingredients

- 1kg beef fillet
- 250g mushrooms, finely chopped
- 4 slices prosciutto
- 1 sheet puff pastry
- 1 egg yolk, beaten
- 1 tbsp Dijon mustard
- 1 tbsp butter
- Salt and pepper

Instructions

1. Sear beef fillet in butter, season, and let cool.
2. Sauté mushrooms until dry.
3. Lay prosciutto on cling film, spread mushrooms, and place beef on top.
4. Roll tightly and chill.
5. Wrap in puff pastry, brush with egg yolk, and chill again.
6. Bake at 200°C (400°F) for 35-40 minutes.

Princess Diana's Bread and Butter Pudding

Ingredients

- 6 slices bread, buttered
- 500ml milk
- 2 eggs
- 50g sugar
- 1 tsp vanilla extract
- 50g raisins

Instructions

1. Preheat oven to 180°C (350°F).
2. Layer bread and raisins in a baking dish.
3. Whisk milk, eggs, sugar, and vanilla, then pour over bread.
4. Bake for 30-35 minutes until golden.

Regal Sticky Toffee Pudding

Ingredients

- 200g dates, chopped
- 250ml boiling water
- 1 tsp baking soda
- 100g butter
- 100g sugar
- 2 eggs
- 150g flour
- 1 tsp vanilla extract

Toffee Sauce:

- 100g butter
- 100g brown sugar
- 150ml cream

Instructions

1. Soak dates in boiling water with baking soda.
2. Cream butter and sugar, add eggs, then mix in flour and vanilla.
3. Stir in date mixture and bake at 180°C (350°F) for 30 minutes.
4. Simmer toffee sauce ingredients and pour over pudding.

The Crown's Mulled Wine

Ingredients

- 750ml red wine
- 1 orange, sliced
- 2 cinnamon sticks
- 3 cloves
- 50g sugar

Instructions

1. Simmer all ingredients in a pot for 10 minutes.
2. Strain and serve warm.

Queen's Garden Mint Pea Risotto

Ingredients

- 200g arborio rice
- 1 small onion, chopped
- 750ml vegetable stock
- 100ml white wine
- 150g peas
- 50g parmesan, grated
- 2 tbsp fresh mint, chopped

Instructions

1. Sauté onion and rice until translucent.
2. Add wine and cook until absorbed.
3. Gradually add stock, stirring frequently.
4. Stir in peas, parmesan, and mint before serving.

Buckingham Palace Fruitcake

Ingredients

- 200g mixed dried fruit
- 100ml brandy
- 200g flour
- 150g butter
- 150g brown sugar
- 3 eggs
- 1 tsp mixed spice

Instructions

1. Soak dried fruit in brandy overnight.
2. Cream butter and sugar, then add eggs.
3. Mix in flour, spice, and soaked fruit.
4. Bake at 160°C (320°F) for 1.5 hours.

The Royal Eton Mess

Ingredients

- 200g strawberries, chopped
- 2 meringue nests, crushed
- 200ml whipped cream

Instructions

1. Fold strawberries and meringue into whipped cream.
2. Serve immediately.

Princess Margaret's Crêpes Suzette

Ingredients

- 125g flour
- 2 eggs
- 300ml milk
- 50g butter
- 1 orange, zested and juiced
- 2 tbsp sugar
- 2 tbsp Grand Marnier

Instructions

1. Whisk flour, eggs, and milk to make a batter.
2. Cook thin crêpes in butter.
3. Melt sugar in a pan, add orange juice, zest, and Grand Marnier.
4. Toss crêpes in sauce and serve warm.

Highgrove Estate Honey & Oat Bars

Ingredients

- 200g rolled oats
- 100g butter
- 100g honey
- 50g brown sugar
- 50g chopped nuts (optional)
- 50g dried fruit (raisins, apricots, or cranberries)

Instructions

1. Preheat oven to 180°C (350°F) and line a baking tray with parchment paper.
2. Melt butter, honey, and sugar in a saucepan over low heat.
3. Stir in oats, nuts, and dried fruit.
4. Press mixture into the prepared tray and bake for 15-20 minutes until golden.
5. Let cool before slicing into bars.

Balmoral Castle Venison Wellington

Ingredients

- 1kg venison fillet
- 250g mushrooms, finely chopped
- 4 slices prosciutto
- 1 sheet puff pastry
- 1 egg yolk, beaten
- 1 tbsp Dijon mustard
- 1 tbsp butter
- 1 tbsp olive oil
- Salt and pepper

Instructions

1. Preheat oven to 200°C (400°F).
2. Sear venison in butter and olive oil, then set aside to cool.
3. Sauté mushrooms until dry.
4. Lay prosciutto on cling film, spread mushrooms over it, and place venison on top.
5. Roll tightly and chill for 15 minutes.
6. Wrap in puff pastry, brush with egg yolk, and bake for 25-30 minutes.

Queen's Champagne and Strawberry Sorbet

Ingredients

- 500g fresh strawberries, hulled
- 100g sugar
- 100ml water
- 1 tbsp lemon juice
- 150ml champagne

Instructions

1. Blend strawberries until smooth.
2. Heat sugar and water in a pan until dissolved, then cool.
3. Mix strawberry purée, sugar syrup, and lemon juice.
4. Churn in an ice cream maker, adding champagne in the last few minutes.
5. Freeze until firm before serving.

King's Coronation Lamb Curry

Ingredients

- 1kg lamb shoulder, diced
- 2 onions, chopped
- 3 garlic cloves, minced
- 1 tbsp ginger, grated
- 2 tbsp curry powder
- 1 tsp ground cumin
- 1 tsp ground coriander
- 400ml coconut milk
- 200ml chicken stock
- 2 tbsp tomato paste
- 1 tbsp olive oil
- Salt and pepper

Instructions

1. Heat oil in a pan, sauté onions, garlic, and ginger until soft.
2. Add spices and cook for 1 minute.
3. Brown lamb pieces, then stir in tomato paste, coconut milk, and stock.
4. Simmer for 1.5-2 hours until tender.
5. Serve with rice and naan.

Queen's Royal Game Pie

Ingredients

- 500g mixed game meat (venison, rabbit, pheasant), diced
- 1 onion, chopped
- 2 garlic cloves, minced
- 1 carrot, diced
- 200ml red wine
- 250ml beef stock
- 1 tsp thyme
- 1 tbsp flour
- 1 sheet puff pastry
- 1 egg yolk, beaten

Instructions

1. Preheat oven to 200°C (400°F).
2. Brown meat in a pan, then remove and set aside.
3. Sauté onion, garlic, and carrot until soft.
4. Stir in flour, add wine and stock, and return meat to the pan. Simmer for 1 hour.
5. Transfer to a pie dish, cover with puff pastry, and brush with egg yolk.
6. Bake for 25-30 minutes until golden.

Crown Jewel Pavlova

Ingredients

- 4 egg whites
- 200g sugar
- 1 tsp white vinegar
- 1 tbsp cornstarch
- 300ml heavy cream, whipped
- 150g mixed berries (strawberries, raspberries, blueberries)
- 1 tbsp powdered sugar

Instructions

1. Preheat oven to 120°C (250°F).
2. Beat egg whites until stiff peaks form, then gradually add sugar.
3. Fold in vinegar and cornstarch.
4. Spread mixture into a circle on a baking sheet and bake for 90 minutes.
5. Cool, then top with whipped cream and berries. Sprinkle with powdered sugar before serving.

Princess Anne's Favorite Kedgeree

Ingredients

- 250g smoked haddock
- 200g basmati rice
- 1 onion, finely chopped
- 2 boiled eggs, chopped
- 1 tbsp butter
- 1 tsp curry powder
- 500ml milk
- 2 tbsp fresh parsley, chopped
- Salt and pepper
- Lemon wedges, to serve

Instructions

1. Poach the smoked haddock in milk for 5 minutes, then flake and set aside.
2. Cook rice according to package instructions.
3. In a pan, melt butter and sauté onion until soft. Add curry powder and cook for 1 minute.
4. Stir in rice, flaked haddock, and chopped boiled eggs.
5. Season, add parsley, and serve with lemon wedges.

Royal Cheese Soufflé

Ingredients

- 30g butter
- 30g flour
- 300ml milk
- 100g mature cheddar, grated
- 3 eggs, separated
- 1 tsp Dijon mustard
- Salt and pepper

Instructions

1. Preheat oven to 200°C (400°F) and butter a soufflé dish.
2. Melt butter in a saucepan, stir in flour, and cook for 1 minute.
3. Gradually add milk, whisking until smooth.
4. Remove from heat, stir in cheese, mustard, and egg yolks.
5. Whisk egg whites to stiff peaks, then fold into the mixture.
6. Pour into the soufflé dish and bake for 20-25 minutes until risen.

Duchess of Cambridge's Pumpkin Soup

Ingredients

- 1 small pumpkin, peeled and chopped
- 1 onion, chopped
- 2 garlic cloves, minced
- 750ml vegetable stock
- 250ml coconut milk
- 1 tsp ground nutmeg
- 1 tbsp olive oil
- Salt and pepper

Instructions

1. Heat oil in a pan, sauté onion and garlic until soft.
2. Add pumpkin, stock, and nutmeg. Simmer for 20 minutes.
3. Blend until smooth, then stir in coconut milk.
4. Season and serve warm.

Windsor Park Asparagus Tart

Ingredients

- 1 sheet puff pastry
- 250g asparagus spears, trimmed
- 150g crème fraîche
- 1 egg yolk
- 50g Parmesan, grated
- Salt and pepper

Instructions

1. Preheat oven to 200°C (400°F).
2. Roll out puff pastry and place on a baking sheet.
3. Mix crème fraîche, egg yolk, and Parmesan. Spread over pastry.
4. Arrange asparagus on top, season, and bake for 20 minutes.

The Royal Family's Christmas Pudding

Ingredients

- 200g suet
- 250g raisins
- 250g currants
- 100g mixed peel
- 100g brown sugar
- 100g flour
- 100g breadcrumbs
- 1 tsp cinnamon
- 1 tsp nutmeg
- 2 eggs
- 150ml stout
- 50ml brandy

Instructions

1. Mix all ingredients and let sit overnight.
2. Transfer to a greased pudding basin.
3. Steam for 4-5 hours, then cool.
4. Reheat by steaming for 2 hours before serving.

Monarch's Heritage Plum Cake

Ingredients

- 250g dried plums (prunes), chopped
- 200g flour
- 150g sugar
- 100g butter
- 2 eggs
- 1 tsp baking powder
- 1 tsp cinnamon
- 100ml milk

Instructions

1. Preheat oven to 180°C (350°F).
2. Cream butter and sugar, then beat in eggs.
3. Fold in flour, baking powder, cinnamon, and milk.
4. Stir in plums, pour into a greased cake tin, and bake for 40-45 minutes.

Queen's Signature Afternoon Tea Blend

Ingredients

- 2 tsp loose Earl Grey tea
- 2 tsp loose Assam tea
- 1 tsp loose Darjeeling tea

Instructions

1. Mix the teas in a jar.
2. Steep 1 tsp per cup in hot water for 3-5 minutes.
3. Serve with milk or lemon, as preferred.

www.ingramcontent.com/pod-product-compliance
Lightning Source LLC
LaVergne TN
LVHW081328060526
838201LV00055B/2511